Character Values

I Am

Tolerant

by Sarah L. Schuette

D1505375

Consulting Editor: Gail Saunders-Smith, PhD
Consultant: Madonna Murphy, PhD
Professor of Education, University of St. Francis, Joliet, Illinois
Author, *Character Education in America's Blue Ribbon Schools*

Capstone
press
Mankato, Minnesota

Pebble Books are published by Capstone Press
151 Good Counsel Drive, P.O. Box 669, Mankato, Minnesota 56002
www.capstonepress.com

1 2 3 4 5 6 09 08 07 06 05 04

Library of Congress Cataloging-in-Publication Data
Schuette, Sarah L., 1976–
    I am tolerant / by Sarah L. Schuette.
    p. cm.—(Character values)
    Includes bibliographical references and index.
    ISBN 0-7368-2573-8 (hardcover)
    1. Toleration—Juvenile literature. [1. Toleration. 2. Conduct of life.] I. Title.
II. Series.
BJ1431.S38 2005
179′.9—dc22   2003024171

Summary: Simple text and photographs illustrate how children can be tolerant.

Note to Parents and Teachers

The Character Values series supports national social studies standards for units on individual development and identity. This book describes tolerance and illustrates ways students can be tolerant. The photographs support early readers in understanding the text. The repetition of words and phrases helps early readers learn new words. This book also introduces early readers to subject-specific vocabulary words, which are defined in the Glossary. Early readers may need assistance to read some words and to use the Table of Contents, Glossary, Read More, Internet Sites, and Index/Word List sections of the book.

Table of Contents

Being Tolerant

I am tolerant. I accept people for who they are. I know that all people are not alike.

I learn about different cultures. I learn how other people eat.

Tolerance at School

My classmate and I do not look the same. But we smile and laugh together.

10

I speak English.
My classmate speaks
Spanish. But we learn
math together.

Family and Friends

I like dogs. My sister likes cats. It is all right that we like different animals.

My friend and I have
different religions.
We learn about each
other's beliefs.

I like baseball.
My friend likes
basketball. So we
play basketball first.

I like pizza. My sister likes hot dogs. I am tolerant when I try food that other people like.

I am tolerant. I listen to new ideas. I accept people who are different than me.

Glossary

classmate—someone who is in the same class as you

culture—a way of life, traditions, ideas, and customs; different places around the world have different cultures; tolerant people are open to learning about new cultures.

religion—a set of spiritual beliefs that people follow

tolerant—being willing to respect or accept the opinions, customs, and beliefs of other people

Read More

Nelson, Robin. *Respecting Others.* First Step Nonfiction. Minneapolis: Lerner, 2003.

Raatma, Lucia. *Tolerance.* Character Education. Mankato, Minn.: Bridgestone Books, 2000.

Scheunemann, Pam. *Tolerance.* United We Stand. Edina, Minn.: Abdo, 2003.

Internet Sites

FactHound offers a safe, fun way to find Internet sites related to this book. All of the sites on FactHound have been researched by our staff.

Here's how:

1. Visit *www.facthound.com*
2. Type in this special code **0736825738** for age-appropriate sites. Or enter a search word related to this book for a more general search.
3. Click on the **Fetch It** button.

FactHound will fetch the best sites for you!

Index/Word List

Word Count: 132
Early-Intervention Level: 13

Editorial Credits
Mari C. Schuh, editor; Jennifer Bergstrom, series designer and illustrator;
  Enoch Peterson, book designer; Karen Hieb, product planning editor

Photo Credits
Capstone Press/Gem Photo Studio/Dan Delaney, all

The author dedicates this book to Wade Miller of Havre, Montana, and Corey Eilers
  of Minneapolis, Minnesota.